150
NEVADA STATE LAW
REAL ESTATE
EXAM QUESTIONS

| JOSEPH R. FITZPATRICK |

150 NEVADA STATE LAW REAL ESTATE EXAM QUESTIONS

Authored by Joseph R. Fitzpatrick
edited by Terrance M. Fitzpatrick

First Edition 2015 091715JF
ISBN-13: 978-1511632584
ISBN-10: 1511632585

Real estate licensing courses and textbooks available through RealtySchool.com:

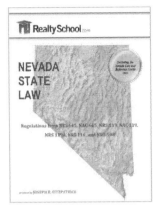

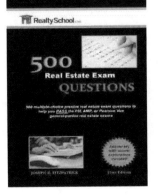

A FEW NOTES FROM THE AUTHOR

Joseph R. Fitzpatrick

About state exams:

Thank you for selecting the RealtySchool.com publication, *150 Nevada State Law Real Estate Exam Questions.* This textbook contains 150 multiple-choice, practice real estate exam questions to help you PASS the PSI *Nevada state-portion* real estate exam.

The various states employ professional testing companies to administer their exams, the most prevalent of which are currently Psychological Services Inc. (PSI), Applied Measurement Professionals (AMP), and Pearson Vue. These testing companies produce a candidate bulletin for each state they service that goes into great detail of registration, center locations, how the computer works, the number of test items, passing scores, and perhaps most important, the exam content outline. Be sure to go to psiexams.com and download the Candidate Bulletin for Nevada real estate licensees.

These testing companies hire any number of test item writers and maintain a bank of several hundred or even several thousand test questions. Many states will randomly select questions from the bank in order to produce an individual exam thus preventing future test takers from knowing all the answers.

How to use this publication:

The questions within this publication are *not* the questions from the actual state examination. In fact, no one really knows what is in a state's bank of questions, so don't let anyone fool you by saying, "That's not on the exam" or "That question will be there for sure." While we don't know any specific questions or answers, we do know the content *topics* and the *types* of questions that you will likely see.

The RealtySchool.com textbook, *150 Nevada State Law Real Estate Exam Questions*, should be used as an additional resource when preparing for your Nevada state exam or even your licensing school's exam, but it is not intended to serve as your main course of instruction.

You might also note that RealtySchool.com has published a number of other titles to help students prepare for both the general and state portions of their respective states and the textbooks have either been approved by the real estate Commission in their states or approval is pending:

- Nationwide Real Estate Pre-licensing Course
- Nationwide Real Estate Pre-licensing Course: Specializing in Florida
- Nationwide Real Estate Pre-licensing Course: Specializing in Alabama
- Nationwide Real Estate Pre-licensing Course: Specializing in Georgia
- Nationwide Real Estate Pre-licensing Course: Specializing in Oklahoma
- Nationwide Real Estate Pre-licensing Course: Specializing in Washington (Fundamentals)
- Nationwide Real Estate Pre-licensing Course: Specializing in Washington (Practices)
- Nationwide Real Estate Pre-licensing Course: Specializing in Utah
- Nationwide Real Estate Pre-licensing Course: Specializing in Kansas (Principles)
- Nationwide Real Estate Pre-licensing Course: Specializing in Kansas (Practices)
- Nevada Real Estate Broker Management Course
- 500 Real Estate Exam Questions

We published the book in such a way that *every* right-hand page contains additional questions while *every* left-hand page provides answers with explanations for the previous page. That way, you can easily go through a page of questions without being tempted to peek at the answers.

We also suggest that you work the questions with some scratch paper to write down your answers rather than marking your book if you want to make another attempt at the questions at a later time.

You can approach the 150 questions in this publication using two different strategies: "bite-size" or "chunk-size." You can answer the questions a page at a time and then turn the page to see how you did. Or, you can go through a block of questions (a "chunk" of 50 or so) and then go back and review the answer key.

As the author, I knew that most students who purchased this textbook will be working the questions without interaction with a licensed real estate instructor. Because of that, I made the extra effort to write an answer key that indicates the correct A, B, C, or D responses, but that also offers explanations as to why the right answer is correct and why some of the wrong "distractors" are incorrect.

I feel that the answer key is more important than the questions. I strongly recommend that even if you got the question right, you should still read the explanation in the key. The answer key can also serve you as a teaching tool as well. You will also see that the statutes and regulations are also referenced in the answer key. I strongly encourage you to read the laws that are associated with each question.

Tips for multiple-choice questions:

1. Most importantly, we recommend that you approach each multiple choice question using this pattern:
    - read the question carefully
    - next, read the distractors (choices A, B, C, and D) carefully
    - next, re-read the question
    - next, make your choice
    - and never come back to the question again

2. Students who go back and change their previous answers, usually change a right answer to a wrong answer.

3. Your first instinct in answering a multiple-choice question is usually right. Your gut reaction is usually right for a number of psychological reasons.

4. Read all the choices before choosing your answer. Don't just recognize one as right and ignore the rest.

5. Think about what your answer would be before looking at the choices, and they likely won't deter you.

6. Don't agonize over one question and waste time you might need to answer several relatively easier ones later in the test. Students have wasted 5 to 10 minutes on a single question, rather than moving on after just a couple of minutes which time could have been spent answering 5 or more other questions correctly.

7. Be sure you are responding to the question that is being asked. Don't inadvertantly create your own question through review of the choices.

8. Answer each question *in order*. If you are stumped, choose an answer you *believe* is correct. The software that the testing companies use allow you to mark a question for review and come back to it if you really feel you should. Interestingly, you may also find something in a subsequent question that will clarify the marked for review question and bring out the answer.

9. Often you are looking for the *most appropriate* choice or *best one* not just one that is right. It needn't be applicable every time in every instance without any exceptions. If two choices appear to be right, there must be a reason one choice is better than the other.

"Test-niques" – These are strategies (a term we made up) to use when you simply do not know the answer or are torn between two answers. We do not want you to utilize these test-niques in lieu of properly preparing for your exam or applying your knowledge. These tips are a last-resort measure which is certainly better than leaving the question blank.

10. Be cautious with distractors containing words like *always, never, only, and must*. Very few things are *always* the case; never say *never*; and you should *only* pick such absolute generalizations if you *must*!

11. Usually the correct answer is the choice with the most information. Often qualifiers and clarifiers are added. In other words, the longest distractor is often the right one.

12. With "all of the above" and "none of the above" choices, if you are certain one of the statements is true, don't choose "none of the above." If you are sure one of the statements is false, don't choose "all of the above."

13. Multiple-choice questions are really four, true-false questions. Read the question with each option applied. Treat each option as a true-false question, and choose the "truest." Mark each question T or F to discover the odd one.

14. Choices that do not match grammatically with the question are often suspect distractors.

15. Distractors that are totally unfamiliar to you are questionable, unlikely, and might be silly or made up terms.

16. Eliminate choices that mean basically the same thing when a single selection is required.

17. On math questions (national portion only), if you perform a calculation, and you see that number *is* a choice, don't just assume that's the answer. Excellent test item writers purposely make calculation errors that we feel students might make, and then we put that miscalculation among the distractors.

19. Use the "hover" technique. Yes, I might be stretching it here, but I did say the test-niques were strategies to try a last resort before simply guessing. Take your fingertip and let it hover between the choices you are considering. Read the question again and let your finger hover over the two distractors while you plug each distractor into the question. Many times, whether it's your subconscious or some other explanation, your finger will stop over the correct choice.

20. There is no such thing as a trick question! Students hate to hear this, but it is true. There must always be a reason it's A and not B even though you might not be able to explain why. "That's a trick question!" is a response students give when they don't know the material thoroughly enough to explain the answer and why the question is really valid.

21. If nothing else works, pick C!!!

Wishing you success:

RealtySchool.com and I have published this collection of real estate exam questions to "condition" you and "get you in shape" for the Nevada real estate licensing exam. We hope you find the publication to be a superb supplement in preparing for your upcoming exam.

Because this is a first edition textbook, I personally invite you to share any feedback by emailing us at support@realtyschool.com. We wish you the very best of success in obtaining your license and enjoying a satisfying career in real estate.

Joseph R. Fitzpatrick

Joe Fitzpatrick graduated from The University of Nevada, Las Vegas (UNLV) and began his career with Coldwell Banker Real Estate. There, he managed the North Miami office and eventually opened Century 21 Fitzpatrick Realty with family. The firm became the top-ranked Century 21 company in Broward County. In 1991, Mr. Fitzpatrick returned to Las Vegas where he began teaching and authoring real estate courses. He also continued on as Vice-President of Century 21 MoneyWorld, which was among the top 10 of Century 21 firms in the world, and led the education division among other duties. Mr. Fitzpatrick joined Real Estate School of Nevada as the Director and currently serves as the Vice President of Education for both Real Estate School of Nevada and RealtySchool.com. He has authored and published over a dozen real estate licensing textbooks and courses that have been approved and are being utilized in several states.

1. A *Seller's Real Property Disclosure* document is required for all of the following properties EXCEPT a(n):

    A. For Sale by Owner.
    B. new home.
    C. resale residence.
    D. home that has been inspected by a certified home inspector.

2. A Nevada licensee must give the *Duties Owed by a Nevada Licensee* form to prospective purchasers or tenants:

    A. before they are shown any properties.
    B. at an open house.
    C. at the close of escrow.
    D. no later than the time of entering an agreement to purchase or lease.

3. The licensing law of Nevada requires that the:

    A. broker keep all information confidential that the seller has provided about the property.
    B. broker disclose everything that the seller tells him or her.
    C. broker disclose information that materially affects the property even when the buyer does not ask for it.
    D. seller disclose all facts that might affect the sale.

4. If a Nevada licensee tells the lender that the sales price on a property is something other than its actual sale price, the:

    A. licensee has done nothing wrong as long as the appraisal substantiates the price.
    B. buyer is likely to receive an interest rate discount.
    C. licensee can have his or her license suspended or revoked.
    D. buyer can receive a lower mortgage amount.

5. Under the terms of the contract, a seller is required to provide a termite certification. The seller requests his listing agent to order one. The agent does so, knowing he will receive a referral fee from the pest control company. Is this a violation of the Nevada license law?

    A. No, if the referral fee is less than $25.
    B. No, because undisclosed referral fees are not a violation of the Nevada license law.
    C. Yes, because a salesperson may not receive compensation from anyone other than his employing broker.
    D. Yes, because only the seller may compensate a salesperson.

1. B. An SRPD is not required on a new home sale. NRS 113.130.

2. D. Hard to find in the licensing law, but the Division's Informational Bulletin #005 says, "It (the *Duties Owed* form) should still be signed as soon as practicable but in no event later than the time of a written contract. **NOTE:** A written contract would include any brokerage agreement including listing agreements, buyer brokerage agreements, property management agreements as well as any purchase agreements and/or conforming lease agreements.

3. C. The broker, or the licensee acting on behalf of the broker, must disclose information that materially affects (material facts) regarding the property even when the buyer does not ask for it. These facts must be disclosed even if it negatively affects the seller or the future of the transaction.

4. C. NRS 645.635 states that the Commission can discipline a licensee for "Representing to any lender, guaranteeing agency or any other interested party, verbally or through the preparation of false documents, an amount in excess of the actual sale price of the real estate or terms differing from those actually agreed upon."

5. C. A broker could receive a referral fee from the pest company if it is disclosed to all parties, but a salesperson or broker-salesperson may not. A salesperson or broker-salesperson may only be compensated by the employing broker. NRS 645.633.

6. All of the following are grounds for disciplinary action EXCEPT a licensee:

    A. trying to negotiate a sale of property directly with an owner while that owner is currently exclusively listed with another broker.
    B. giving information on a rental to a tenant without the landlord's permission.
    C. refusing to write a low offer that the licensee knows will not be accepted.
    D. refusing to show property to a prospective purchaser due to poor credit.

7. What are the three types of agency recognized in Nevada?

    A. single agency, dual agency, and assigned agency
    B. seller agency, buyer agency, assigned dual agency
    C. subagency, dual agency, seller agency
    D. fiduciary agency, universal agency, multiple agency

8. A broker may collect a commission from both the seller and the buyer only if:

    A. the broker is a dual agent.
    B. the buyer and the seller are at non-arm's length.
    C. both parties give their informed, written consent.
    D. both parties have legal representation.

9. A Nevada real estate salesperson, associated with Hammond Realty, who wishes to put her own house on the market for sale and place a sign on the property must:

    A. identify the broker on the sign and it may identify the salesperson.
    B. identify both her name and the brokerage name.
    C. identify her name and contact information.
    D. indicate her status as a REALTOR®.

10. All funds received by the broker on behalf of the principal must be deposited in the trust account or escrow opened:

    A. within three days of receiving the offer.
    B. within 10 business days of execution of the contract.
    C. within five calendar days of receiving the offer.
    D. within one banking day of acceptance of the offer.

6. D. Refusing to show property because of the client's credit status is not illegal and in fact, is good business practice. The other acts are prohibited under NRS 645.630-635.

7. A. NRS 645.252 and NRS 645.254

8. C. If the licensee receives compensation from more than one party in a real estate transaction, full disclosure to and consent from each party to the real estate transaction is required. A licensee shall not accept compensation from more than one party in a real estate transaction, even if otherwise permitted by law, without full disclosure to all parties. NAC 645.605. The broker need not be a dual agent. Do not associate compensation with agency representation.

9. A. A for sale sign is considered to be advertising. The name of a brokerage firm under which a real estate broker does business or with which a real estate broker-salesperson or salesperson is associated must be clearly identified with prominence in any advertisement. NAC 645.610. If a licensee is a real estate broker-salesperson or real estate salesperson, the licensee shall not advertise solely under the licensee's own name when acting in the capacity as a broker-salesperson or salesperson. All such advertising must be done under the direct supervision of and in the name of the brokerage with whom the licensee is associated. NRS 645.315.

10. D. If a real estate broker receives money, as a broker, which belongs to others, the real estate broker shall promptly deposit the money in a separate checking account located in a bank or credit union in this state which must be designated a trust account. NRS 645.310. "Promptly" is considered to be one business day.

11. Broker-Salesperson Harrigan accepts an earnest money deposit from his buyer, payable to his brokerage, when writing the offer. Under Nevada law, Harrigan must:

    A. deposit the money in his trust account immediately.
    B. hold the check in a secure location until acceptance of the offer, then open escrow.
    C. deposit the funds in a separate trust account solely for that transaction.
    D. turn the funds over to his broker promptly.

12. Salesperson Harriet engages in blockbusting and discriminatory activities and also deposited an earnest money check in her personal checking to purchase a new car. Harriet's broker, John, was completely unaware of these activities. What is the impact of Harriet's behavior on John when the violations are brought before the Commission?

    A. John may be disciplined for failure to supervise.
    B. John is liable for Harriet's actions, but not Harriet, as she is only a salesperson.
    C. John will be disciplined only for violations of the Fair Housing Act.
    D. John must surrender his license.

13. Several weeks after the close of escrow, a broker-salesperson received a nice thank you note with a bonus check from the seller. The broker-salesperson cashed the check and kept the funds for her own use. Which of the following is TRUE?

    A. This is a violation of Nevada regulations and the broker-salesperson may be disciplined.
    B. This is perfectly legitimate, but only if the check were payable to the broker-salesperson.
    C. This is acceptable provided the broker is aware.
    D. This is legal as long as the bonus check is not in excess of $500.

14. Every Nevada real estate office is required to keep transaction records for:

    A. three years from last activity.
    B. five years from last activity.
    C. seven years from last activity.
    D. none of the above

15. Regarding time share promotional meetings:

    A. Division employees may attend.
    B. recording devises are not allowed.
    C. verbal statements may enhance written advertising.
    D. shills are permitted.

11. D. Every real estate salesperson or broker-salesperson who receives any money on behalf of a broker or owner-developer shall pay over the money promptly to the real estate broker or owner-developer. NRS 645.310.

12. A. Every real estate broker shall teach the licensees associated with him or her the fundamentals of real estate or time-share practice, or both, and the ethics of the profession. The broker shall supervise the activities of those licensees, the activities of his or her employees and the operation of his or her business. NAC 645.600. The Commission may suspend, revoke or deny the renewal of the license of a real estate broker and may assess a civil penalty of not more than $5,000 against the broker if it appears he or she has failed to maintain adequate supervision of a salesperson or broker-salesperson associated with the broker and that person commits any unlawful act or violates any of the provisions of NRS 645. NRS 645.660.

13. A. A salesperson or broker-salesperson may only receive compensation from the employing broker. NRS 645.280.

14. B. The broker must keep the transaction files for 5 years from the last activity and those files must be kept at a location approved by the Real Estate Division. NAC 645.650.

15. A. NAC 119.510 allows investigators and other employees of the Division to attend any promotional meeting, and requires all verbal statements to be consistent with written statements that are on file with the Division, and prohibits the use of shills. Recording devices are actually allowed but their use must be disclosed. NAC 119.510.

16. Who is responsible for investigating transaction files and trust records of brokers and owner-developers?

    A. the Nevada Real Estate Commission
    B. the Attorney General
    C. the Division interloper
    D. The Administrator and the Division

17. Three weeks before Nick begins his real estate pre-licensing course, he offers to help his neighbor sell her house. The neighbor agrees to pay Nick a 5% commission. An offer is accepted while Nick is still taking the course and closes the day after he passes the PSI exam. The neighbor then refuses to pay Nick the commission. Can Nick sue to recover payment?

    A. No. Only the broker can sue for commissions.
    B. No. State law prohibits the suit since Nick was unlicensed at the time of listing.
    C. Yes. Nick performed under the listing agreement.
    D. Both A&B

18. Chandler is being disciplined. What was NOT the reason?

    A. calling himself a "REALTOR®" without belonging to the Association of REALTORS®
    B. guaranteeing future profits to a buyer when he resells
    C. acting as a principal in a transaction
    D. a fraudulent action in real estate sales prior to his licensing in Nevada

19. An owner-developer may employ all of the following EXCEPT:

    A. a licensed salesperson.
    B. a licensed broker-salesperson.
    C. a licensed broker.
    D. an unlicensed host or hostess.

20. Which of the following could result in the suspension, revocation, or fine in an exclusive right to sell listing agreement?

    A. a specified commission rate
    B. no broker protection clause
    C. no specific termination date
    D. no automatic renewal clause

16. D. This is the responsibility of the Administrator as an agent for the Division. NRS 645.195.

17. D. There was no listing agreement that we know of. Nick would have to be licensed in order to perform real estate services for his neighbor, for compensation. Only the broker can sue for commissions as any agreement for compensation would have to be with the client and the broker.

18. C. The licensee can act as a principal provided he or she discloses the license status and that he or she is a principal. All of the other choices are prohibited under NRS 645.630-635.

19. C. Salespersons and broker-salespersons work for brokers or owner-developers. Brokers do not work for others.

20. C. Every exclusive agency representation agreement is required to be in writing and have a clearly defined expiration date. NRS 645.320.

21. The Farmers listed their house for sale with Broker Simmons on February 1st. The listing was to last 6 months. In April, the Farmers decided they no longer wanted to sell the property. Which of the following statements is TRUE?

    A. The sellers have ended the listing agreement and there are no penalties.
    B. The sellers have in effect withdrawn the broker's right to sell and may be liable to the broker.
    C. The Farmers are required to leave the house on the market until July 31st.
    D. The sellers are liable for a commission if the broker sells the property after the withdrawal of the listing.

22. A buyer has just entered into a contract to buy a condominium unit from a person who originally purchased the unit from the developer and has lived there for the last 10 years. The buyer has a statutory right to cancel the contract within:

    A. 3 business days
    B. 5 days of the contract date.
    C. 10 days of receipt of the certificate of resale.
    D. There is no right of cancellation

23. All of the following contracts must be in writing EXCEPT:

    A. exclusive agency listing
    B. open listing
    C. exclusive right to sell listing
    D. real estate sales contract

24. A California broker wants to broker lots in Nevada to California investors. The California broker may do this if he:

    A. relocates to Nevada.
    B. obtains a cooperative certificate.
    C. pays a Nevada broker a referral fee.
    D. This cannot be done.

25. All of the following are requirements of a property manager permit holder EXCEPT:

    A. 24 hours of pre-permit education.
    B. 3 hours of continuing education in property management.
    C. a real estate license.
    D. a broker's license.

21. B. The best answer is B; the sellers have in effect withdrawn the broker's right to sell and may be liable to the broker. Regarding choices A and D, the sellers *could* be liable to the broker for expenses or a commission if the property is sold at a later date – the terms of the listing termination (withdrawal) would dictate the seller's potential liability for such. The sellers, however, do not have to keep the property on the market.

22. D. Although there are some rights of rescission with respect to time shares, subdivided land sales, and membership campgrounds in 119, 119A, and 119B, there is no right of rescission in the typical new home or resale transaction. The buyer may be able to cancel after reviewing the certificate of sale but this would have to be a provision in the contract. It is not a statutory right.

23. B. Exclusive agency agreements must be in writing per NRS 645.320. Open listings may be oral or in writing. Real estate contracts must also be in writing per Nevada law.

24. B. NAC 645.180-185.

25. D. The educational requirement for the property management permit is 24 hours. There is a 3-hour continuing education course requirement in property management. A property management permit can be issued to a qualified salesperson, broker-salesperson, or broker. NRS 645.6052.

26. Who MUST have a real estate license?

    A. the owner of the property being sold or leased
    B. an executor of an estate
    C. a bankruptcy trustee
    D. a property manager

27. A Nevada licensee had her Arizona license suspended for failure to account and commingling. She:

    A. may have her Nevada license suspended because of the Arizona suspension.
    B. will NOT be disciplined in Nevada for the Arizona offense.
    C. will automatically have her Nevada license suspended.
    D. does not have to disclose the Arizona incident to the Real Estate Division of Nevada.

28. Which of the following MAY have an active Nevada real estate license?

    A. depository financial institution
    B. Division employee
    C. suspended licensee
    D. nonresident of Nevada

29. In Nevada, a partnership, association, or corporation will be granted a Nevada real estate license only if:

    A. there is a member who meets the qualifications of a broker.
    B. every member actively participating in the brokerage business has a broker's license.
    C. all papers are filed with the Secretary of State
    D. all of the above

30. In Nevada, an unlicensed assistant may perform all of the following activities EXCEPT:

    A. compute commission checks.
    B. assemble disclosure documents required for a closing.
    C. explain simple contract documents to prospective purchasers.
    D. prepare mailings and promotional materials.

26. D. A property manager must hold a real estate license. The other three choices are exemptions under NRS 645.240.

27. A. The Commission may take action pursuant to <u>NRS 645.630</u> against a person who is subject to that section for the suspension or revocation of a real estate broker's, broker-salesperson's or salesperson's license issued by any other jurisdiction.

28. D. Non-residents of Nevada may have an active license provided they meet Commission prescribed requirements. A Division employee is prohibited from having an active license (NRS 6435.130). A suspended licensee's license will be on inactive status, not active. A depository financial institution is also prohibited from having a license (NRS 645.335).

29. A. In Nevada, a partnership, association, or corporation will be granted a Nevada real estate license only if there is a member who meets the qualifications of a broker. NRS 645.370.

30. C. Explaining documents and contracts to clients is an act which requires a license. The other activities are acceptable for an unlicensed assistant to perform.

31. Brown, a nonresident of Nevada, applies for a Nevada broker-salesperson's license. She must file with the Division a:

   A. Certificate of Habitability.
   B. Consent to Service of Process.
   C. Certificate of Resale.
   D. Corpus Delicti.

32. A Nevada broker may have his license suspended or revoked for all of the following EXCEPT:

   A. failing to keep adequate records.
   B. depositing earnest money directly into the firm's trust account.
   C. helping a student cheat on the licensing exam.
   D. displaying a for sale sign on a property without the authorization of the owner.

33. In Nevada, real estate commissions are:

   A. limited by the real estate Division.
   B. determined by a group of prominent brokers.
   C. set by what is customary and has always been the norm.
   D. negotiable between the client and the broker.

34. A net listing in Nevada is:

   A. illegal.
   B. advisable.
   C. permissible with approval of the Division.
   D. permissible if the seller understands and agrees.

35. How are members of the Commission selected to serve?

   A. chosen by the Council on Housing Matters (CHM)
   B. appointed by the Nevada Governor
   C. elected through public elections
   D. hand-picked by HUD

31. B. No license may be issued pursuant to <u>NRS 645.490</u> to a resident of a state other than Nevada until the applicant has appointed in writing the Administrator to be his or her agent, upon whom all process, in any action or proceeding against the applicant, may be served. NRS 645.495.

32. B. The very purpose of a trust account is for the deposit of earnest money. It should be obvious, then, that this would not be a violation of licensing laws.

33. D. Real estate commissions must be negotiated between the client and the broker. The Real Estate Division certainly has no say or influence on a broker's fee. Commissions are not determined by a group of prominent brokers or that would be collusion and prohibited under anti-trust laws. According to anti-trust laws, there is no "norm."

34. D. Nevada courts have ruled that net listings are permissible if the seller understands and agrees. They are not advisable as these situations often create a conflict of interest with the seller and the brokerage.

35. B. Commissioners are appointed by the Governor. NRS 645.050.

36. The Nevada Real Estate Commission consists of:

    A. four active real estate brokers or broker-salespersons and one public member.
    B. a combination of licensees and members of the public.
    C. five actively licensed brokers or broker-salespersons.
    D. five actively licensed brokers or salespersons.

37. Who may receive compensation from ERRF?

    A. a broker whose commission was refuted by his client
    B. a seller who pays a commission to a broker under false pretenses
    C. a buyer who paid a brokerage fee under a brokerage agreement
    D. a cooperating agency which did not receive its share of the commission from the listing firm

38. What is the maximum fine for a violation of NRS 645.630, NRS 645.633, or NRS 645.635 (the major violations)?

    A. $500 per offense
    B. $5,000 per offense
    C. $10,000 per offense
    D. $20,000 per offense

39. Salesman Clem tells his clients not to worry about the air conditioning unit in the house they are buying. "This entire house was checked out from head to toe two weeks ago by a licensed inspector." Although Clem was told this by the seller, and Clem was just repeating what the seller told Clem, Clem is presumed guilty of:

    A. misrepresentation.
    B. fraud.
    C. twisting.
    D. all of the above

40. Agent Denise accepts an earnest money check from her purchasers, the Smithers, in the amount of $2,000 to accompany an offer they wish her to present to the bank. Denise, in some financial trouble, deposits the money in her own checking account to pay some bills knowing she will be able to replace the funds after her next closing due to close the following week.

    A. Denise may do so legally provided she replaces the funds immediately after her next closing.
    B. Denise must hold up on presenting the offer to the bank as there is no earnest money to accompany the offer.
    C. Denise, but not her broker, can be disciplined as this is conversion.
    D. none of the above

36. C. The Commission consists of five actively licensed brokers or broker-salespersons. NRS 645.050, NRS 645.090.

37. B. ERRF will not settle the non-payment of commissions. There is no evidence to suggest that the broker did anything unlawful in choice C.

38. C. Presently, a violation could lead to a disciplinary action of a fine of $10,000, plus suspension or revocation of the license.

39. A. This is misrepresentation as it was innocent in nature and Clem was repeating what he had been told by the seller. It is, therefore, not fraud. "Twisting" is a licensee's interference with another brokerage's brokerage agreement with a client.

40. D. Denise may only turn the funds over to her employing broker promptly. All monies received by a salesperson or broker-salesperson must be turned over to the employing broker "promptly." Promptly is understood to be one business day. The salesperson may not keep the money or any portion of it. NRS 645.310.

41. Wilcox is applying for a license as a broker. Which of these in NOT required?

    A. Wilcox's business location and any fictitious names to be used
    B. 3-year work history
    C. statement of Wilcox's previous real estate experience, if any
    D. disclosure of any past felony convictions or real estate license suspension or revocation

42. A real estate broker, representing a seller, knows the house has a cracked foundation and that the husband committed suicide in the house. The broker must disclose:

    A. neither fact.
    B. both facts.
    C. the suicide but not the foundation.
    D. the foundation but not the suicide.

43. The licensing law of Nevada requires that when a broker represents both parties in the same transaction, the broker shall obtain the written consent of all parties. That written consent must:

    A. contain a description of the transaction.
    B. include a statement that the licensee has a conflict of interest.
    C. state that the licensee is representing multiple parties with adverse interests
    D. all of the above

44. The listing salesperson is showing his listing to very interested buyers. The asking price is $249,000. The salesperson suggests to the buyers that hey make an offer of $230,000 because the salesperson believes that might be accepted by his sellers. Has the salesperson violated the licensing law?

    A. No, because he is representing the buyers whenever he writes an offer on their behalf.
    B. No, because the salesperson is attempting to generate some sort of purchasing activity on the property.
    C. Yes, because he offered the property at a price not authorized by the sellers and is breaching his fiduciary duty.
    D. Yes, because the offer is not a bona fide offer.

45. Broker Mark procures a ready, willing, and able buyer for his seller. The seller accepts the offer in writing and then experiences a change of heart 3 days later and withdraws his acceptance. In this situation, Mark:

    A. cannot collect a commission as the transaction will not close.
    B. may sue the buyer.
    C. may well be entitled to collect a commission.
    D. may retain the deposit in lieu of a commission.

41. B. A person may not be licensed as a real estate broker unless the person has been actively engaged as a full-time licensed real estate broker-salesperson or salesperson in this State, or actively engaged as a full-time licensed real estate broker, broker-salesperson or salesperson in another state or the District of Columbia, for at least 2 of the 4 years immediately preceding the issuance of a broker's license. NRS 645.330.

42. D. Circumstances associated with "stigmatized" properties, such as a murder or suicide took place in the house, are not considered to be material facts in Nevada as well as most other states. A cracked foundation is a material fact as it is a construction defect, and it must be disclosed.

43. D. These requirements are included in the *Consent to Act* form. NRS 645.252.

44. C. The listing agent's suggestion to the buyer or the buyer's agent of a price the seller would be willing to accept other than the list price is prohibited (unless the seller has given authorization for the listing agent to do so). NRS 645.635.

45. C. A broker has earned a commission upon producing a ready, willing, and able buyer.

46. A seller's listing agreement has expired, and the seller lists with a different brokerage. Jim, the original listing agent, now has a buyer interested in the seller's property. Jim:

   A. must be an assigned agent.
   B. cannot disclose to the buyer information about the physical condition of the property.
   C. cannot represent the buyer due to his prior relationship with the seller.
   D. cannot disclose to the buyer offers received on the seller's property or an acceptable selling price to the seller.

47. Which of the following types of agency is NOT recognized in Nevada?

   A. single agency
   B. assigned agency
   C. dual agency
   D. transaction brokerage

48. Salesperson Judy has been working with buyers to find their dream home. After locating a property, the buyers ask Judy if she can recommend a home warranty program. Judy knows of a company who will pay a referral fee for referring them. Can Judy make this recommendation?

   A. No. This is illegal per Nevada licensing law.
   B. No, if Judy's broker has an alliance with a home warranty company.
   C. Yes, if Judy discloses the referral fee, and it is paid through her broker.
   D. Yes, if the home warranty company is the cheapest.

49. The city of Belmont, Nevada requires a city real estate license before any compensated real estate activity is allowed in that city. Is this legal?

   A. Yes, but only for revenue purposes such as business license.
   B. Yes, and Belmont may require schooling and a separate test for certification.
   C. No, because the state of Nevada has jurisdiction superseding Belmont.
   D. No, because the additional regulation by a city would be redundant.

50. Paul, an associate with Hummingbird Realty, lists a property with seller Fitzsimmons. After discussing it with his wife, Paul decides he and his wife would like to purchase the property themselves from Fitzsimmons. As a Nevada licensee, Paul:

   A. must be a dual agent.
   B. cannot purchase his own listing as it is a conflict of interest.
   C. must maintain his duties as the sellers' agent.
   D. must be a buyer's agent only and have his broker re-assign the listing and arrange for seller representation.

46. D. After the termination or revocation of a brokerage agreement, the licensee shall not disclose confidential information relating to a client for 1 year. That implies that the fiduciary duty ends after one year. NRS 645.254.

47. D. Transaction brokerage is not recognized in Nevada. NRS 645.252, NRS 645.253.

48. C. If a licensee refers a client to another company such as a home warranty company, the nature of the referral must be disclosed to the client. NAC 645.605. A salesperson or broker-salesperson may only receive compensation from the employing broker. NRS 645.630.

49. B. Local cities have the authority to require separate licensing requirements and to regulate the practices of licensees. NRS 645.250

50. D. The licensee can certainly purchase his own listing, but he would then be looking out for his own best interests instead of the seller's. It is therefore not possible for him to represent the seller in any way, thus eliminating dual agency or seller agency.

51. Broker A enters into a listing with the seller. Salesperson B learns of the listing through the MLS and finds a buyer ready, willing, and able to purchase. Typically in Nevada, Salesperson B:

    A. is a sub-agent to Broker A.
    B. and the buyer will enter into a buyer brokerage agreement together.
    C. must represent both the seller and the buyer.
    D. has a fiduciary to the buyer.

52. What is the purpose for the *Consent to Act* form?

    A. the parties to the transaction acknowledge and agree to a dual agency transaction.
    B. to spell out the actions the agent will provide to the client and the client's consent to the same.
    C. the fiduciary's consent for the broker to act on the client's behalf.
    D. all of the above

53. Salesperson Jeanette paid the local newspaper company to run an ad in the real estate section. Jeanette's ad promotes "Jeanette Sells Vegas" including her accomplishments, production awards, market share, and contact information. Jeanette must also include in the ad:

    A. the registered name of her brokerage firm.
    B. her real estate license number.
    C. the wording, "This ad approved by the Nevada Real Estate Division."
    D. all of the above

54. Every Nevada real estate office is required to keep transaction records pertaining to:

    A. sales that closed.
    B. transactions that failed to close.
    C. offers that were rejected.
    D. all of the above

55. Broker-salesperson Adam hires a marketing firm to design a web site to promote Adam's real estate career. Which of the following omissions from the web site could result in a fine from the Nevada Real Estate Division?

    A. the brokerage name.
    B. Adam's cell phone number.
    C. pictures of the properties Adam wishes to advertise.
    D. none of the above

51. D. Typically in Nevada, the brokerage that finds a buyer for another firm's listing, represents the buyer, and commonly a buyer brokerage agreement is executed. However, the brokerage agreement is between the buyer and the broker – not the salesperson.

52. A. Do not assume the "all of the above" or "none of the above" choices are always correct! The only accurate statement is choice A, that the *Consent to Act* is utilized so the parties to the transaction can acknowledge and agree to a dual agency transaction. NRS 645.253. Choice B refers to the *Duties Owed* form, not the *Consent to Act*.

53. A. The name of a brokerage firm under which a real estate broker does business or with which a real estate broker-salesperson or salesperson is associated must be clearly identified with prominence in any advertisement. NAC 645.610.

54. D. A broker must keep transaction files for 5 years from the last activity and those files include close transactions, transactions that did not close, and offers that were not accepted. NAC 645.650.

55. A. A web site is treated like any other advertisement and the name of the brokerage firm must be clearly identified with prominence. NAC 645.610.

56. What is the most standard real estate brokerage commission in Las Vegas?

    A. 3%
    B. 4%
    C. 6%
    D. none of the above

57. Which of the following statements is TRUE regarding an earnest money deposit?

    A. Cash is not permitted.
    B. A promissory note is illegal in Nevada.
    C. An earnest money deposit of some sort is legally required with an offer.
    D. It can be anything of value that is acceptable to the offeree.

58. In Nevada, must a Broker maintain a trust account?

    A. Yes.
    B. Yes and the account information must be on file with the Commission.
    C. No, only if the Division has exempted the broker from maintaining one.
    D. No.

59. Broker Clayton has opened a brokerage and will handle earnest money. Which is FALSE?

    A. She may have several trust accounts.
    B. She is the trustee of the trust account.
    C. The Real Estate Division cannot inspect her trust account records without a complaint from a consumer first.
    D. She must notify the Division of the banks where she has trust accounts.

60. Broker Wilson writes "TBD" in the blank field for expiration date of his listing agreement with seller McKinley. Which of the following is TRUE?

    A. Wilson has violated a Nevada statute as every listing must have a specific termination date.
    B. Wilson could be disciplined by the Nevada Real Estate Commission.
    C. Wilson could be fined as much as $10,000 and have his license suspended or revoked.
    D. all of the above

---

56. D. Per anti-trust laws, there is no standard brokerage fee.

57. D. Regarding earnest money deposits, cash is certainly permitted, but caution should be used in handling and accounting. A promissory note is legal, but may be worthless. An earnest money deposit is not legally required, but is common. The only true statement is that the earnest money deposit can be anything of value that is acceptable to the offeree. NRS 645.630.

58. D. NAC 645.175.

59. C. The Real Estate Division can inspect a broker's transaction of trust account records at any time, even without a complaint from a consumer.

60. D. Failure to include a fixed date of expiration in any written brokerage agreement is grounds for disciplinary action per NRS 645.633.

61. In Nevada, a real estate salesperson may lawfully collect a commission from:

    A. either the buyer or the seller as long as the correct agency disclosure is made.
    B. the salesperson's broker.
    C. a licensed title or escrow firm registered in Nevada.
    D. all of the above

62. Broker Johnson is in the process of opening a branch office in Sparks, Nevada. Johnson applies for a branch office license and clearly identifies the relationship with his main office. The broker appoints salesperson Kelly as the branch office manager. Which of the following is TRUE?

    A. Kelly must be a resident of Sparks.
    B. Johnson will be granted a branch office license as he has named a branch office manager.
    C. Johnson cannot promote his Las Vegas listings in Sparks.
    D. Johnson's application will be denied.

63. Beyond the initial licensing period, a Nevada real estate license expires every:

    A. 48 months.
    B. 24 months.
    C. 30 months.
    D. 15 months.

64. In Nevada, in order for a listing broker to sue for a commission, all of the following are necessary for her to show entitlement for that commission EXCEPT:

    A. there was a brokerage agreement.
    B. the property successfully closed escrow.
    C. the broker produced a ready, willing, and able purchaser who met price and terms acceptable to the seller.
    D. The broker was properly licensed at the time of procurement.

65. The three most prominent brokers in the valley meet and discuss their brokerage practices. Which of the following can the brokers agree to do?

    A. to divide the valley in three geographic areas and agree that each broker will confine his business to his area, refraining from doing business in the others
    B. to charge only a commission rate of 7%
    C. to refuse to cooperate and share commissions with CENTURY 21 firms
    D. none of the above

61. B. Choice A is tempting, but it is the *broker* who can collect a commission from either the buyer or the seller, not the salesperson. The salesperson can only collect a commission from the employing broker. NRS 645.633.

62. D. The application for the branch office will be denied because the broker is appointing a salesperson to be the branch manager. A branch manager must be a broker or a broker-salesperson who, within the preceding 4 years, has had 2 years of active experience NAC 645.177.

63. B. The initial license period for an original license as a real estate broker, broker-salesperson or salesperson is a period of 12 consecutive months beginning on the first day of the first calendar month after the original license is issued by the Division. Thereafter, each subsequent license period is a period of 24 consecutive months beginning on the first day of the first calendar month after a renewal of the license is issued by the Division for the subsequent license period. NRS 645.780 references the former rules. The Division changed this effective July 15, 2015.

64. B. A broker is said to have earned a commission when that broker procures a ready, willing, and able buyer to meet the price and terms acceptable to the seller. That broker must be actively licensed at the time of procurement and authorized for the payment of a commission under a brokerage agreement. The transaction need not close escrow for the broker to be entitled.

65. D. All of the choices are in violation of anti-trust laws. Market allocation, price fixing (commission setting), and boycotting are specific violations.

66. Regarding signage for a Nevada real estate brokerage firm, the broker must have a sign:

     A. unless the brokerage activities will be conducted in her home.
     B. at the main office with identical signs at any branch offices.
     C. with letters of at least 5 inches in height.
     D. visible from the nearest public sidewalk, street, or highway, on the building directory, or at the entry of the business.

67. James Wickitt has offices in nine western states including Nevada. He is the broker to over 7,600 licensed associates. If any, one, associate in any, one, location makes a misrepresentation to a client, Wickett:

     A. may be disciplined for failure to supervise.
     B. should have offered better training and management.
     C. cannot be disciplined because he would have no way to know of the misrepresentation.
     D. will have his license suspended until a monetary fine is paid.

68. A broker must disclose all of the following to the Nevada Real Estate Division within 10 days of their occurrence EXCEPT:

     A. a change of address for the brokerage.
     B. the termination of a licensee.
     C. a name change of the brokerage such as the addition of a franchise name.
     D. completion of mandatory continuing education courses.

69. Which of the following continuing education courses is NOT required for a broker-salesperson to renew his license:

     A. property management
     B. broker management
     C. agency relationships
     D. law and ethics

70. In Nevada, an unlicensed assistant may perform all of the following activities EXCEPT:

     A. typing and filing.
     B. assemble documents and organize files.
     C. tell prospective clients the prices and details of homes advertised for sale.
     D. order termite, roof, and general property inspections.

66. D. All sign requirements are listed in NAC 645.615.

67. A. Every real estate broker shall teach the licensees associated with him or her, the fundamentals of real estate or time-share practice, or both, and the ethics of the profession. The broker shall supervise the activities of those licensees, the activities of his or her employees and the operation of his or her business. NAC 645.600. The Commission may suspend, revoke or deny the renewal of the license of a real estate broker and may assess a civil penalty of not more than $5,000 against the broker if it appears he or she has failed to maintain adequate supervision of a salesperson or broker-salesperson associated with the broker and that person commits any unlawful act or violates any of the provisions of NRS 645. NRS 645.660.

68. D. A change of address for the brokerage, the termination of a licensee, or a name change of the brokerage all require notification to the Division within 10 days of their occurrence. There is no need to notify the Division of the completion of a continuing education course until it is time to submit your C.E. certificates.

69. A. A property management continuing education course *could* be taken by a broker-salesperson for credit, but it is not required unless the licensee is a property management permit holder.

70. C. Quoting prices and details of homes is an act of selling which requires a license. The other activities are acceptable for an unlicensed assistant to perform.

71. Common Interest Community documents are:

    A. only required on new construction.
    B. required to be provided by the association which may charge a reasonable fee.
    C. due by the close of escrow.
    D. always paid for by the seller.

72. Williams has been interviewed by Dream Properties for a registered representative position.

    A. Williams must pass an examination.
    B. Williams is allowed to sell only under the strict supervision of a broker for the first 90 days.
    C. Williams will receive a license.
    D. Williams may only induce attendance at an offering or sales promotion and cannot sell.

73. Hustlin' Harry is desperately looking for listings in his farm area. In an attempt to get a quick listing, he door knocks and tells the homeowners that a particular ethnic group is buying all the homes in the neighborhood.

    A. Harry is creating "panic selling."
    B. Harry is "blockbusting."
    C. Harry may be fined and have his license suspended or revoked.
    D. all of the above

74. Broker Greenfield accepted an exclusive-right-to-sell listing. Which of these is FALSE regarding this listing?

    A. It must be in writing.
    B. It must have a fixed termination date.
    C. It cannot have an automatic renewal clause.
    D. It does not need Greenfield's signature to be enforceable.

75. In Nevada, the age of legality is:

    A. 17
    B. 18
    C. 21
    D. none of the above

71. B. The CIC docs are applicable in any transaction where an HOA exists. The contract dictates when the docs must be delivered to the buyer for review, and it is certainly before the close of escrow. Who pays the fee for the docs is negotiable, although it is common that the seller pays.

72. D. NRS 119.181.

73. D. These acts are prohibited under the federal Fair Housing Act. The licensee's activities would likely be treated as "any other conduct which constitutes deceitful, fraudulent or dishonest dealing" and therefore punishable under NRS 645.633.

74. D. The listing does require broker Greenfield's signature to be enforceable. That is the false statement. The other statements are all true statements.

75. B. This question is not really a Nevada real estate law question, but it is important to know that the age of majority in Nevada is 18. Also, NAC 645.100 states that an applicant for a license as a real estate salesperson must be at least 18 years of age.

76. Edwards is an applicant for an original Nevada salesperson's license. Edwards must complete:

    A. a course in appraisal.
    B. 15 classroom hours of Nevada law.
    C. 64 semester units of college coursework.
    D. a 90-hour approved pre-licensing course.

77. Waiver of pre-licensing educational requirements for brokers and broker-salespersons is made for active, full-time experience as follows:

    A. 15 credits for every two years.
    B. 16 credits for every two years.
    C. 8 credits for every one year.
    D. There is no waiver for experience.

78. A Nevada real estate salesperson is having trouble getting her practice started. She and her boyfriend agree that she will pay him to cold call, and she will pay him $75 for each listing appointment he sets and $65 for each buyer appointment he sets. Is there anything wrong with this arrangement?

    A. No, cold calling is a common practice in real estate.
    B. No, and only she needs a real estate license.
    C. No, the amount is below the $100 limit.
    D. Yes, this is a license requiring activity, and payment can only be made from brokers to licensees.

79. In Nevada, when must a broker provide the parties to a transaction with a closing statement?

    A. at the time of closing
    B. within one business day before close of escrow
    C. never
    D. within 10 business days after close of escrow

80. Homeowner Smithers refuses to show his house for rent to any members of African descent. Upon being refused an opportunity to preview the house because of their ethnicity, the Thompsons file a complaint with the Nevada Real Estate Division. Upon confirmation of the discrimination, the Division will:

    A. start a formal investigation to affirm or deny the allegations.
    B. issue an injunction against Smithers.
    C. assist the Thompsons with a legal suit against Smithers.
    D. do nothing, as the Division has no jurisdiction over an unlicensed person.

76. D. NAC 645.435.

77. B. Each person who holds a license as a real estate broker, broker-salesperson or salesperson, or an equivalent license, issued by a state or territory of the United States, or the District of Columbia, is entitled to receive credit for the equivalent of 16 semester units of college level courses for each 2 years of active experience that, during the immediately preceding 10 years, the person has obtained while he or she has held such a license, not to exceed 8 years of active experience.

78. D. The actions of the boyfriend fall into the categories of soliciting and selling of real estate and real estate services as well as receiving bonuses for appointments set. To be compensated in this manner, a real estate license is required. NRS 645.230-235, 633.

79. D. The requirement is within 10 business days after the closing although the title company's (escrow holder) delivery of a HUD-1 fulfills this broker requirement. NRS 645.635.

80. D. The Real Estate Division will not get involved as this is a private transaction not involving a real estate licensee.

81. A license may be suspended or revoked for any of the following EXCEPT:

    A. being arrested for the possession of illegal drugs.
    B. a plea of guilty to a felony.
    C. having a license suspended or revoked in another state.
    D. commingling.

82. Stevens is a vice-president for a corporation which often acquires, and then needs to sell, homes in its regular course of business. Because of his extensive real estate knowledge, the company has Stevens handle the real estate transactions as a part of his job description. Which of the following statements is TRUE?

    A. Stevens must have a real estate license.
    B. Stevens doesn't need a real estate license, but does need to register with the Division.
    C. As long as Stevens does this as a part of his job, without special compensation, he does not need a real estate license in Nevada.
    D. Stevens can acquire and sell the properties on behalf of the company and receive special compensation for doing so.

83. When must the *Seller's Real Property Disclosure* statement be provided to the buyers?

    A. within 4 working days of closing
    B. as soon as practical, but no later than the signing of the sales contract
    C. never, if the buyers are allowed to inspect the home
    D. at least 10 days before the property is conveyed to the purchaser

84. Your seller is home while you are showing your listing to your buyer prospect. You hear the seller make a statement which you know is incorrect regarding the condition of the roof. You should:

    A. do nothing, as you didn't make the statement.
    B. take the seller aside and tell him not to say that.
    C. do nothing, as the seller made a good faith mistake.
    D. find the party to whom the statement was made and provide the correct information.

85. Golden Gate is a gated community of estate homes. It is regulated by an HOA with very restrictive CC&Rs. Your buyers have found a home in Golden Gate and are ready to submit an offer. Before you ask them to sign the offer, you must:

    A. present the buyer's application to the HOA for approval to become owners.
    B. provide them with a CIC disclosure form and other papers regarding the extent and nature of restrictions at Golden Gate.
    C. provide them with the Certificate of Resale package.
    D. do nothing more. It is up to the buyers to decide if Golden Gate is for them.

81. A. Being *arrested* for any offense is not grounds for license revocation; being *convicted*, is. The other choices are all grounds for revocation of license. NRS 645.630-635.

82. C. A corporation which, through its regular officers who receive no special compensation for it, performs any of those acts with reference to the property of the corporation, is exempt from licensure. NRS 645.240.

83. D. The disclosure must be delivered to the buyers no later than 10 days before the property is conveyed to the purchaser (close of escrow) NRS 113.

84. D. Representations about the soundness of the roof are material facts and must be true and correct. The licensee has the obligation to correct the information that was provided to the purchasers. NRS 645.254.

85. B. Nevada licensees have to provide the disclosure "BEFORE YOU PURCHASE PROPERTY IN A COMMON-INTEREST COMMUNITY DID YOU KNOW . . ." according to NRS 116. The Certificate of Resale package need not be presented to the buyers before the contract is entered into, but the contract will be contingent upon the buyer's approval of the documents within a specified number of days from acceptance.

86. Your buyer wants you to write an offer at $245,000, on a property listed at $299,000. You advise them that such a low offer might easily offend the seller. Your buyer feels the offer will uncover if the seller is willing to come down on the price. You must:

     A. follow your instinct and write an offer nearer to the asking price.
     B. write the offer at $245,000.
     C. tell the seller that you were required to write the offer, but the buyer was seeking to uncover how much the seller would come down on the price.
     D. refuse to write the offer as it is ridiculously low.

87. An advance fee agreement:

     A. must be in writing.
     B. cannot apply to marketing fees.
     C. requires a written accounting of all funds within 60 days from receipt of funds.
     D. can allow the licensee to charge additional sums for rendering the original services to be provided if the costs are more than anticipated by the licensee.

88. Broker Jeff's salesperson asks him, "Are there any situations where the *Duties Owed by a Nevada Licensee* does not apply?" Jeff would be correct if he replied:

     A. "A *Duties Owed* is not required on a sale where a licensee represents both the seller and the buyer because a *Consent to Act* will be utilized."
     B. "A *Duties Owed* is not required on a sale where a licensee represents either the seller or the buyer, and the other party is unrepresented."
     C. "A *Duties Owed* is not required on the sale of corporeal personalty."
     D. "A *Duties Owed* is not required where a licensee is acting as a principal in the transaction."

89. McCullough has left Kemp Realty and his license has been returned to the Division. How much time does McCullough have to affiliate with another broker before his license is inactivated?

     A. 10 days
     B. 15 days
     C. 30 days
     D. No time is allowed at all.

90. Susan writes an offer with the buyer on Saturday, emails the offer to the listing agent on Saturday night, and receives a signed acceptance Monday afternoon. What is the requirement of her handling the buyer's earnest money deposit?

     A. She must turn it over to her broker no later than the close of business, Monday.
     B. She must give her broker or the escrow company the check no later than Tuesday.
     C. She must give her broker or the escrow company the check no later than Thursday.
     D. She must turn the deposit over to her broker the same day she wrote the offer.

86. B. As a licensee, you could be disciplined for failure to reduce a bona fide offer to writing when the purchaser requests that of you. NRS 645.635.

87. A. Advance fees can, and usually do, apply to marketing fees. An accounting of the expenditures of the advanced fee must be provided to the principal within 3 months of use of the money. The agreement must be in writing. NRS 645.322.

88. C. "Corporeal personalty" is fancy language for tangible, personal property such as a washer and dryer. This is not the sale of real property so there is no *"Duties Owed"* form required. The other transactions require the form.

89. C. The former broker has to submit a termination notice and the salesperson's license to the Division or sign to allow the salesperson to hand carry it to the Division. This must be done within 10 days of the termination. The licensee then has 30 days to affiliate with the new broker, but must not partake in activities requiring a license until a receipt is issued by the Division for the payment of fees and the request to transfer brokers. NRS 645.580.

90. B. A licensee who receives a deposit on any transaction in which he or she is engaged on behalf of a broker or owner-developer shall pay over the deposit to that broker or owner-developer, or to the escrow business or company designated in the contract, within 1 business day after receiving a fully executed contract. NAC 645.657.

91. A claim has been paid from the ERRF to satisfy a judgment against Slater. Which of these is TRUE?

    A. Slater's license will automatically be revoked.
    B. All rights of the claimant must be subrogated to the Attorney General.
    C. Before Slater can reinstate, he must repay the sum paid from ERRF plus 6% interest.
    D. Before Slater can reinstate, he must repay ERRF payments plus interest at 2% over prime rate.

92. A buyer has purchased land regulated under NRS 119. She has what period time to cancel the contract and have any monies returned if she changes her mind for any reason?

    A. 5 days
    B. 15 days
    C. 30 days
    D. There is no right to cancel.

93. Broker Barrett receives an earnest deposit from one of his salespeople on Friday at 2:00 pm on an offer that has met the listed price and terms. Barret MUST:

    A. keep the money since the firm has procured a ready willing and able buyer.
    B. keep only the money which will be his commission.
    C. deposit the funds by the end of the day, Friday.
    D. deposit the funds into his trust account the following Monday.

94. Of the following licensees, Dan, Betty, and Hector, who had to submit proof of 64 college credits unless waived by full-time, active real estate experience?

    A. salesperson Dan
    B. salesperson Dan and broker Betty
    C. broker-salesperson Hector and broker Betty
    D. only broker Betty

95. Georgia has three years of previous, active, full-time real experience in Virginia, and is making application in Nevada to be a broker. Which of these is TRUE?

    A. She may have 32 college credits waived.
    B. She may have the 18 hour Nevada law requirement waived.
    C. She may have the three semester units of broker management education waived.
    D. none of the above

91. D. If the Administrator pays from the ERRF fund any amount in settlement of a claim or towards satisfaction of a judgment against a licensee, the licensee's license issued must be automatically *suspended* (not revoked) upon the effective date of an order by the court authorizing payment from the fund. The license may not be reinstated until he or she has repaid in full, plus interest at a rate equal to the prime rate at the largest bank in Nevada plus 2 percent until the judgment is satisfied. NRS 645.847.

92. A. The purchaser of any subdivision or any lot, parcel, unit or interest in any subdivision, not exempted under the provisions of NRS 119.120 or 119.122 may cancel, by written notice, the contract of sale until midnight of the fifth calendar day following the date of execution of the contract, and the contract must so provide. The right of cancellation may not be waived. NRS 119.182.

93. D. NRS 645.630 states that upon acceptance of an agreement, in the case of a broker, failing to deposit any check or cash received as earnest money before the end of the next banking day unless otherwise provided in the purchase agreement, is a violation. The broker *could* deposit the funds on Friday, be he *MUST* deposit the funds no later than the close of business the following Monday.

94. C. An applicant for an original real estate broker's or broker-salesperson's license must furnish proof satisfactory to the Real Estate Division that the applicant has completed 64 semester units or the equivalent in quarter units of college level courses. NRS 645.343.

95. D. An applicant for an original real estate broker's or broker-salesperson's license must furnish proof satisfactory to the Real Estate Division that the applicant has completed 64 semester units or the equivalent in quarter units of college level courses. Each person who holds a license as a real estate broker, broker-salesperson or salesperson, or an equivalent license, issued by a state or territory of the United States, or the District of Columbia, is entitled to receive credit for the equivalent of 16 semester units of college level courses for each 2 years of active experience that, during the immediately preceding 10 years, the person has obtained while he or she has held such a license, not to exceed 8 years of active experience. (This does not get prorated. Even though she has three years of experience, she only gets 16 credits waived.) This credit may not be applied against the requirement in subsection 2 for three semester units or an equivalent number of quarter units in broker management or 18 classroom hours of the real estate law of Nevada. NRS 645.343.

96. Nevada real estate commissioners:

    A. must have been residents of the state of Nevada for a minimum of two years.
    B. must be Nevada-licensed salespersons, broker-salespersons, or brokers.
    C. must be Nevada brokers of three years or broker-salespersons of five years .
    D. are appointed by the Administrator.

97. Which of the following statements is TRUE regarding the powers of the Commission with respect to an unlicensed person?

    A. The Commission has no authority to take disciplinary action against an unlicensed person.
    B. The Commission may impose a fine of up to $5,000 if an unlicensed person performs acts which require a license.
    C. The Commission may suspend, revoke or fine an unlicensed person for performing acts which require a license.
    D. The Commission may not discipline a party who assists an unlicensed individual in performing acts which require a license.

98. A Nevada licensee may prepare a broker's price opinion for a fee provided:

    A. it contains a statement that clarifies the opinion is not an appraisal.
    B. the broker is ultimately responsible for supervising the licensee's preparation of the report.
    C. the licensee discloses any existing or contemplated interest in the property.
    D. all of the above

99. A licensee who acts as an agent in a real estate transaction shall disclose:

    A. to each party any material and relevant facts.
    B. each source from which the licensee will receive compensation.
    C. that the licensee is a principal to the transaction or has an interest in a principal to the transaction.
    D. all of the above

100. A Nevada licensee who has entered into a brokerage agreement to represent a client in a real estate transaction:

    A. must keep all confidential information confidential forever.
    B. shall present all offers to the opposing party prior to the expiration date of the offer.
    C. shall disclose to the client material facts of which the licensee has knowledge unless the client waives this right.
    D. shall advise the client to obtain advice from an expert relating to matters which are beyond the expertise of the licensee.

96.   C. Commissioners must have been residents of Nevada for at least five years, not two. Salespersons cannot be commissioners. They are appointed by the Governor, not the Administrator. Commissions must be Nevada brokers for at least three years or broker-salespersons for at least five years NRS 645.050, NRS 645.090.

97.   B. The Commission *does have* authority to take disciplinary action against an unlicensed person and may impose a fine of up to $5,000 if an unlicensed person performs acts which require a license. Since the individual has no license, the Commission may *not* suspend or revoke (since there is no license to suspend or revoke), but may fine an unlicensed person for performing acts which require a license. Further, the Commission *may* discipline a party who assists an unlicensed individual in performing acts which require a license. NRS 645.235.

98.   D. All of the statements are true. NRS 645.2515

99.   D. All of the statements are true. NRS 645.252

100. D. Nevada licensees only have an obligation of confidentiality for up to one year after the expiration of the brokerage agreement. Offers must be presented as soon as practicable. The licensee cannot wait until the offer's expiration date. The client cannot waive the rights entitled to under the provision. NRS 645.254.

101. Agent Thomas has delivered his seller client's SRPD to the buyer's agent which concealed the fact that the property had a history of severe pest infestation. Thomas had no knowledge of the prior problems, however was sued along with the seller by the buyer upon discovery of the issues when a new infestation emerged. Will Thomas likely be found liable for the seller's concealment of the pest infestations?

   A. Yes, because Thomas should have known through the exercise of due diligence.
   B. Yes, because Thomas is responsible to verify the information conveyed in the SRPD.
   C. No, because Thomas is not liable for his client's misrepresentation if Thomas had no knowledge of the matter.
   D. No, because Thomas is not expected to have expertise in the field of pest infestation.

102. In Nevada, it is unlawful for a real estate licensee to deny a party to participate in a residential transaction because of any of the following EXCEPT:

   A. sexual orientation.
   B. gender.
   C. familial status.
   D. credit.

103. A Nevada licensee applicant from another state is not required to take or pass the national portion of the state exam provided:

   A. the applicant holds an *active* license in the other state.
   B. the other state's educational requirements are comparable to those of Nevada.
   C. the applicant's license is in good standing with that state's licensing authority.
   D. all of the above

104. Unless extended for further investigation, the Division has how long to act on an applicant's application for licensure?

   A. 30 days
   B. 45 days
   C. 60 days
   D. 90 days

105. Terry is the broker of record. Terry does not have a property management permit, but one of his salespeople, Doris, does. In order for the firm to conduct property management services:

   A. Terry must appoint Doris as the designated property manager with the Division.
   B. Doris must have both an active real estate license and a property management permit.
   C. Doris must have at least two out of the last four years of active experience in property management.
   D. all of the above

101. C. A licensee may not be held liable for a misrepresentation made by his or her client unless the licensee knew the client made the misrepresentation and failed to inform the person to whom the client made the misrepresentation that the statement was false. NRS 645.259

102. D. Refusing to work with a client due to poor credit is not unlawful. To do so for any of the other choices is unlawful discrimination. Note that Nevada includes sexual orientation as a protected class where the federal Fair Housing Act does not. NRS 645.321.

103. D. NRS 645.332.

104. B. 60 days. NRS 645.420.

105. D. NRS 645.6055.

106. Which of the following statements is TRUE regarding the hearing process pertaining to a licensee facing a disciplinary action?

    A. The hearing must be scheduled within 60 days of the filing of the complaint by the Administrator.
    B. The Commission must send written notice of its final decision to the licensee within 30 days after the hearing.
    C. If the decision of the Commission is in favor of the licensee the decision is final.
    D. If the license is revoked, no license will be issued to the licensee within 10 years of the date of revocation.

107. Silvia carelessly failed to renew her Nevada real estate license before the license expiration date. Which of the following statements is TRUE?

    A. She must reapply for a license as an original, first-time applicant.
    B. She may renew her license if she completes additional education requirements.
    C. She may renew her license within one year if she pays additional fees.
    D. She may only renew her license with both the completion of additional education and the payment of additional fees.

108. Which of the following statements is TRUE regarding a business broker's permit in Nevada?

    A. An applicant for an original permit must demonstrate the completion of a 24-hour approved course in business brokerage.
    B. The renewal of the permit must include a 3-hour approved course in business brokerage.
    C. The expiration date of the permit coincides with the expiration date of the licensee's real estate license.
    D. all of the above

109. Nevada law defines "commercial real estate" as being:

    A. improved real estate that consists of not more than four residential units.
    B. unimproved real estate for which more than four residential units may be constructed.
    C. a single-family residential unit, including a condominium or townhouse.
    D. none of the above

110. Which of the following statements is FALSE regarding branch offices?

    A. a branch office must be issued a separate license in the same name as the firm's main office.
    B. a branch office must only be managed by the broker.
    C. a branch office must be under the supervision of a broker or a broker-salesperson who, within the preceding 4 years, has had 2 years of active experience.
    D. A branch office is not required to maintain a trust account.

106. C. The hearing must be scheduled within 90 days of the filing of the complaint by the Administrator, not 60. The Commission must send written notice of its final decision to the licensee within 60 days after the hearing, not 30. If the license is revoked, no license will be issued to the licensee within 1 year of the date of revocation, not 10. NRS 645.680-770.

107. C. She may renew her license within one year of the expiration date if she pays additional fees. NRS 645.785.

108. D. The requirements for a business broker permit and property management permit are similar, if not identical. NRS 645.863.

109. B. Nevada law *negatively* defines "commercial real estate" as NOT being improved real estate that consists of not more than four residential units; unimproved real estate for which not more than four residential units may be developed or constructed pursuant to any zoning regulations or any development plan applicable to the real estate; or a single-family residential unit, including a condominium, townhouse or home within a subdivision, if the unit is sold, leased or otherwise conveyed unit by unit, regardless of whether the unit is part of a larger building or parcel that consists of more than four units. NRS 645.8711.

110. B. NAC 645.175-178.

111. State exam results are accepted by the Division for what period of time from the day of passing the examination?

    A. 30 days
    B. 6 months
    C. 1 year
    D. 18 months

112. Which of the following statements is TRUE regarding a Nevada licensee's first year holding an active real estate license?

    A. She must complete an approved, 45-hour post licensing course.
    B. She must complete an approved, post licensing course either online or in a classroom setting.
    C. She may count certain pre-licensing hours toward the post licensing requirement.
    D. She may have the post licensing requirement waived if the licensee holds a license in another state.

113. Franklin is working toward completing his continuing education requirements. Which of these statements is TRUE?

    A. Franklin must submit 24 hours of approved continuing education courses every two years.
    B. Franklin must submit a minimum of six hours in personal development courses.
    C. Franklin must show a minimum of six hours of agency and six hours of Nevada law.
    D. If Franklin is a broker-salesperson, he must also show six hours in broker management.

114. What is the purpose of creating an "advisory committee" per NAC 645.490-500?

    A. to assist the Administrator or Commission on educational and investigative matters
    B. to advise licensees on legal matters and assist with questions they may have
    C. to provide consumers with guidance in the event of a potential complaint
    D. to recommend new laws and regulations to the Commission for its consideration

115. Broker Rick owns a "100% shop" where all of his licensees pay a nominal monthly fee and receive 100% of their commissions. Because the commission schedule favors the associates, Rick does not offer any training, does not review the transaction files, nor does he have policies and procedures manuals or independent contractor agreements with his associates. Which of these statements is TRUE?

    A. This might not be the best way to run a firm, but Rick is not violating any regulations.
    B. Rick is not required to offer training or to review transaction files.
    C. Rick is required to train and supervise, have a policies a procedures manual, and maintain independent contractor agreements.
    D. Rick is only required by regulation to supervise his sales associates.

111. C. NAC 645.220

112. D. It is a 30-hour requirement, not 45. The course must be a live course, not online. Pre-licensing hours do not count toward the post-licensing requirement. The requirement for post licensing education does not apply to a first-year licensee who holds a real estate license issued by another state or territory of the United States, or the District of Columbia, on the date on which the first-year licensee obtains a real estate license issued by the State of Nevada. NAC 645.4442.

113. A. It is true that Franklin must submit 24 hours of approved continuing education courses every two years. Of the courses Franklin submits, he may have no more than three hours in personal development courses. Franklin must show a minimum of three hours of agency and three hours of Nevada law. If Franklin is a broker-salesperson, he must also show three hours in broker management.

114. A. NAC 645.490-500.

115. C. NAC 645.600.

116. Diane Anderson, Bob Blake, Frederick Caruso, and Sheila Bernheisen have formed a team working for broker Harriet Smith at Lincoln Realty, Inc. Which of the following is permissible pertaining to advertising by the team?

    A.   The team advertises as "The Anderson Team."
    B.   The team advertises as "The Lincoln Realty Team."
    C.   The team advertises as "Diane's Superstars."
    D.   none of the above

117. The broker's sign must be:

    A.   in a conspicuous place upon the premises of the broker's place of business.
    B.   readable from the nearest public sidewalk, street or highway.
    C.   posted on the building directory or on the exterior of the entrance to the business if in an office building.
    D.   all of the above

118. The location of the broker's office must:

    A.   not be in the broker's home.
    B.   not be in an office in conjunction with another business.
    C.   comply with local zoning ordinances.
    D.   be in an office building.

119. A Nevada licensee who acts as a principal in a transaction:

    A.   must disclose his license status.
    B.   must confirm his license status in or by attachment to the contract.
    C.   must disclose his license status as soon as practical but before a contract is entered into.
    D.   all of the above

120. Mary has her mother's house listed for sale. Mary is the agent of her mother, Linda Johnson. Which of the following statements would be best for Mary to disclose?

    A.   "Mary Adams is a Nevada real estate licensee representing the seller."
    B.   "Mary Adams is the agent of the seller, her mother."
    C.   "Mary Adams is a Nevada real estate licensee and is an agent of the seller, Linda Johnson, the mother of Mary Adams."
    D.   None of these are required to be disclosed to the buyer or buyer's agent.

116. A. The team name must contain the last name of one of the team members. "The Lincoln Realty Team" is too similar as to how the brokerage firm might advertise. NAC 645.611.

117. D. NAC 645.615

118. C. The office could be in the broker's home or in conjunction with another business provided the office meets the requirements of NAC 645.627.

119. D. In each real estate transaction involving a licensee, as agent or principal, the licensee shall clearly disclose, in writing, to his or her client and to any party not represented by a licensee, the relationship of the licensee as the agent of his or her client or the status of the licensee as a principal. The disclosure must be made as soon as practicable, but not later than the date and time on which any written document is signed by the client or any party not represented by a licensee, or both. The prior disclosure must then be confirmed in a separate provision incorporated in or attached to that document and must be maintained by the real estate broker in his or her files relating to that transaction. NRS 645.637.

120. C. A licensee shall not acquire, lease or dispose of any time share, real property or interest in any time share or real property for himself or herself, any member of his or her immediate family, his or her firm, or any member thereof, or any entity in which the licensee has an interest as owner unless the licensee first discloses in writing that he or she is acquiring, leasing or disposing of the time share or property for himself or herself or for a member, firm, or entity with which the licensee has such a relationship and He or she is a licensed real estate broker, licensed real estate broker-salesperson or licensed real estate salesperson, whether his or her license is active or inactive. This disclosure may be accomplished with a reference to himself or herself as an agent, licensee, salesperson, broker or broker-salesperson, whichever is appropriate. NAC 645.640.

121. A broker's sign is not in compliance with Nevada regulations. How long does the broker have to rectify the situation?

    A. 3 business days
    B. 10 days
    C. 2 weeks
    D. 30 days

122. What is a significant difference between a broker and an owner-developer?

    A. A broker receives a license; an owner-developer does not.
    B. The broker is regulated by the Division; the owner-developer is not.
    C. A licensee associated with an owner-developer may not be associated with any other broker.
    D. A broker must comply with the provisions of NRS 645 and NAC 645; an owner-developer does not.

123. Real Estate Commissioners may serve a maximum of:

    A. 2 years.
    B. 4 years.
    C. 5 years.
    D. 6 years.

124. A Nevada salesperson's first license was issued on November 3, 2015. When will his license expire?

    A. December 31 of every odd-numbered year
    B. November 30, 2016
    C. October 31 of each odd-numbered year
    D. November 30, 2019

125. A real estate license is required for all of the following activities *EXCEPT:*

    A. managing real estate as an employee for an owner.
    B. reselling a mobile home and the land that goes with it.
    C. selling condominium units.
    D. managing properties for multiple clients.

121. B. Any "deficiencies" must be corrected in 10 days. NAC 645.690.

122. A. A broker receives a license; an owner-developer does not. Both a broker and an owner-developer are regulated by the Division. A licensee associated with either an owner-developer or a broker may not be associated with any other broker or owner-developer (not a difference between a broker and owner-developer). A broker and an owner-developer must comply with the provisions of NRS 645 and NAC 645.

123. D. Commissioners may serve no more than 6 years after which time they are not eligible for appointment or reappointment until 3 years have elapsed from any period of previous service. NRS 645.060.

124. B. Effective July 1, 2015, the first license expires after one year and every two years after that. Licenses expire the last day of the month, the same month as the license was issued. NRS 645.780.

125. A. Managing real estate as an employee for an owner would fall into the category of "persons to whom this chapter shall not apply." NRS 645.240.

126. A Nevada broker is listing a single-family home and asks the seller to complete a Seller's Real Property Disclosure. Which of the following statements is *TRUE?*

      A. The disclosures are optional, and the seller may avoid liability by refusing to make any disclosures about the condition to the property.
      B. The listing agent should fill out the disclosure document if the seller is unwilling.
      C. An agent should advise the seller to omit any known property conditions.
      D. Nevada law requires the seller to disclose any and all known property conditions.

127. Lucy wants to sell her own house with no agent. Lucy:

      A. is required to supply a copy of the *Seller's Real Property Disclosure* form.
      B. is exempt from having to fill out a *Seller's Real Property Disclosure* form because she is not using a real estate agent.
      C. may have someone else complete the form for her.
      D. may sell her house by herself without supplying a *Seller's Real Property Disclosure* form.

128. Sasha wants to sell her own house which is in a common interest community association. Which of the following statements is *TRUE?*

      A. She is required to supply a resale package to the buyer whether or not a broker is used.
      B. In Nevada, anyone who sells his or her own real estate does not need to supply a certificate of resale.
      C. Sasha is required to pay for the resale package.
      D. She may sell her house without any further liability to the buyer regarding a resale certificate.

129. When must a *Seller's Real Property Disclosure* form be delivered to the buyer?

      A. no later than ten days before the property is conveyed to the purchaser
      B. at the time that the seller agrees to the offer
      C. at the time of the home inspection
      D. at the time of closing

130. The seller's agent is required to disclose to potential buyers:

      A. there are spirits haunting the house.
      B. the hot water heater is not working.
      C. there was a death in the home.
      D. the home was occupied by a person with AIDS.

126. D. It is required by law that the seller complete the SRPD. The listing agent should not fill out the form. Any known defects in the property must be disclosed in the document. NRS 113.

127. A. A seller must submit a completed SRPD whether a broker is utilized or not. NRS 113.

128. A. The seller of a property located in a CIC is required to provide the buyer with the certificate of resale. Who pays for the package is negotiable. This is a seller's responsibility regardless of whether a broker is used. NRS 116.

129. A. The disclosure must be delivered to the buyers no later than 10 days before the property is conveyed to the purchaser (close of escrow) NRS 113.

130. B. The fact that the hot water heater is not working is a material fact and must be disclosed. The other items may "stigmatize" the property but are not considered material facts.

131. The Real Estate Division has made available a booklet that contains all the disclosures that must be made per federal, state, and local laws and regulations regarding a residential transaction. This booklet is called:

    A. *Seller's Real Property Disclosure*
    B. *Real Property Disclosure Guide*
    C. *Residential Disclosure Guide*
    D. *Did You Know?*

132. The *Consent to Act* form is required in which of the following situations?

    A. A seller hires you to sell his home. Another broker's buyer purchases it.
    B. You sell your listing to a buyer you also represent.
    C. Your buyer wants to write an offer on a property listed by another agent in your firm.
    D. All of the above

133. The following items must be disclosed to all parties in the transaction as soon as practicable EXCEPT:

    A. a change in the licensee's relationship to a party
    B. a change in the condition of the home being purchased
    C. each source from which the broker will receive compensation
    D. the seller's motivation for selling and the buyer's reasons for buying

134. The seller and the seller's agent are not aware of a problem with the heating system. This would be considered a:

    A. latent defect.
    B. material defect.
    C. patent defect.
    D. stigma.

135. Every purchaser of a time share unit from a developer must be provided with:

    A. a copy of the developer's permit to sell time share units.
    B. the public offering statement.
    C. a copy of the signed contract.
    D. all of the above

131. C. The booklet is called the Residential Disclosure Guide. NRS 645.194.

132. B. The *Consent to Act* form is required in a dual agency (also called multiple party representation) scenario. Choice C is not a dual agency situation. It is an assigned agency.

133. D. Motivation for selling or buying is confidential. The other items must be disclosed.

134. A. Latent defects are those defects that are not visible. These may be known or unknown to the seller or agent. Patent defects are visible.

135. D. NRS 119A.400.

136. During a promotional meeting, what is the maximum number of salespeople who may attempt the sale?

    A. 1
    B. 2
    C. 3
    D. 5

137. When must a salesperson submit the paperwork on a new transaction to his broker?

    A. within 48 hours of a signed purchase agreement
    B. no later than the date on which escrow is opened
    C. within 5 calendar days of all paperwork being signed by all parties
    D. no later than the close of escrow

138. In Nevada, a broker's price opinion must include:

    A. a statement as to the purpose of the opinion.
    B. a statement that it is an opinion of value and is not an appraisal.
    C. the name of the real estate broker.
    D. all of the above

139. Which of the following is FALSE regarding advertising on the internet or social media?

    A. All internet and social media advertising must be done under the supervision of the broker.
    B. The name of the brokerage firm must be predominant in size.
    C. An agency relationship between client and broker can be created by clicking an acceptance box.
    D. All rules of advertising as per NRS 645 apply to advertising on the internet or through social media.

140. When advertising one of your listings, in any media, it is required to:

    A. include the name of the seller in the advertisement.
    B. include the list price in the advertisement.
    C. include your name and phone number in the advertisement.
    D. include the name of your brokerage firm in the advertisement.

136. B. The maximum number of salespeople who can attempt the sale is 2. This is called a takeover attempt. NAC 119.510.

137. C. NAC 645.650 states that a salesperson or broker-salesperson must provide any paperwork to the broker with whom he or she is associated within 5 calendar days after that paperwork is executed by all the parties. Note that the broker could establish a more restrictive policy.

138. D. A broker's price opinion must contain all 3 items and more. NRS 645.2515.

139. C. The false statement is C. An agency relationship between client and broker *cannot* be created by clicking an acceptance box. All the rules and regulations within NRS 645 apply to advertising on the internet and through social media. NAC 645.613.

140. D. All advertising must include the name of the brokerage firm which must be predominant in size. NAC 645.610.

141. Regarding the location of transaction records, a broker:

    A. may keep the records out of state.
    B. must notify the Division within ten days after moving the records to another location.
    C. must notify the Division before moving records to a new location.
    D. may not ever move the records.

142. The maximum amount an individual may claim from the recovery fund pertaining to any one transaction is actual damages but no more than:

    A. $25,000.
    B. $50,000.
    C. $100,000.
    D. $300,000.

143. A security deposit on a rental property may be:

    A. equal to one month's rent.
    B. no more than three months' rent.
    C. required to be in the form of a surety bond.
    D. all of the above

144. When a licensee prepares a written brokerage agreement, authorizing the licensee to purchase or sell real estate for compensation or commission, the licensee shall deliver a copy of the written brokerage agreement to the client:

    A. immediately.
    B. immediately upon signing or a reasonable time thereafter.
    C. within 5 business days.
    D. within 10 days.

145. Enrico, a resident of California, wishes to obtain a Nevada broker-salesperson's license. Enrico may do so provided he:

    A. obtains a $25,000 surety bond.
    B. obtains a cooperative certificate from a Nevada broker.
    C. appoints the Administrator to receive due process.
    D. joins the local association of REALTORS®.

141. C. The real estate broker shall give written notice to the Division of the exact location of the records of the real estate broker and shall not remove them until he or she has delivered a notice which informs the Division of the new location. NAC 645.655.

142. A. when any person obtains a final judgment in any court of competent jurisdiction against any licensee or licensees pursuant to this chapter, upon grounds of fraud, misrepresentation or deceit with reference to any transaction for which a license is required pursuant to this chapter, that person, upon termination of all proceedings, including appeals in connection with any judgment, may file a verified petition in the court in which the judgment was entered for an order directing payment out of the Fund in the amount of the unpaid actual damages included in the judgment, but not more than $25,000 per judgment. The liability of the Fund does not exceed $100,000 for any person licensed pursuant to this chapter, whether the person is licensed as a limited-liability company, partnership, association or corporation or as a natural person, or both. The petition must state the grounds which entitle the person to recover from the Fund. NRS 645.844.

143. D. NRS 118A.242

144. B. NRS 645.300.

145. C. NRS 645.495.

146. What educational requirement must a time share applicant satisfy to be eligible to receive a time share license?

   A. 14 hours
   B. 30 hours
   C. 45 hours
   D. 90 hours

147. A person who violates any provisions of NRS 645 is guilty of a:

   A. tort.
   B. crime of moral turpitude.
   C. gross misdemeanor.
   D. felony.

148. Can a Nevada licensee fulfill all of his continuing education requirements online?

   A. Yes, provided the courses include 3 hours of agency, 3 hours of law or legal update, 3 hours of contracts, and 3 hours of ethics.
   B. Yes, as long as all of the school's online courses have been approved by the Commission.
   C. No, Nevada does not permit continuing education online.
   D. No, at least 50% of the continuing education requirement must be taken in a live, classroom environment.

149. Owner developers must:

   A. complete 48 hours of continuing education every 4-year period.
   B. complete 24 hours of continuing education every 2-year period.
   C. pass the broker's test.
   D. none of the above

150. A broker who offers asset management services:

   A. must disclose any agreements to the Division annually.
   B. must provide evidence to the Division annually that the broker has complied with asset management regulations.
   C. is subject to disciplinary actions including suspension of license and a fine.
   D. all of the above

146. A. The requirement is 14 hours. NRS 119A.210.

147. C. A person who violates any other provision of this chapter, if a natural person, is guilty of a gross misdemeanor, (and if a limited-liability company, partnership, association or corporation, shall be punished by a fine of not more than $2,500.)

148. D. At least 50% of the continuing education requirement must be taken in a live, classroom environment. The continuing education hours for a first renewal is 12 hours and all 12 hours must be live. This is on top of the 30-hour post licensing requirement.

149. D. It is none of the above as owner developers are not licensed. They must register with the Division, but there is no test or continuing education required.

150. D. NRS 645.256.

Made in the USA
San Bernardino, CA
15 January 2016